A Guide to
Microwave Cooking

400 tested microwave recipes, illustrated with over 650 color photos and step-by-step cooking techniques.

All recipes for this book were
prepared and tested in
microwave ovens under the
supervision of professional
home economists.

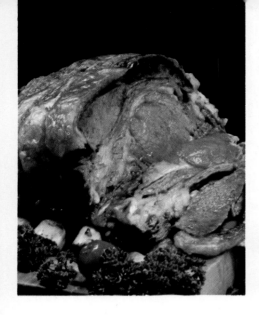

Microwave Cooking is a New Way to Cook

Easy, modern cooking with old-fashioned goodness — your new microwave oven offers the best of both these worlds.

Now you're standing at the threshold of a whole new cooking experience. Microwave cooking is different. You've spent years mastering cooking techniques, and now you're going to have just a few new skills to learn. Techniques, timing, utensils and even the recipes are different than those you learned to cook with on conventional ranges and ovens.

But relax! It's really quite simple. This new microwave cooking guide takes you step by step through a multitude of tried and tested recipes that incorporate any new skills you need to learn. Tucked in with the recipes, you'll discover cooking tips with extra pointers. And microwave cooking is so much fun and so quick, you'll be a master microwave chef in no time at all.

Before you get started, put your best foot forward by studying the owner's guide and operating instructions that came with your microwave oven. Next, spend a little time reading the opening sections of this book which fully explain the uniqueness of microwave cooking. Then select your recipes and get cooking!

POWER LEVEL REFERENCE CHART

Power Levels used in the recipes	Equivalent Settings on various Selector Controls	Power Level Settings on Touch Controls
HIGH (100%)	NORMAL	*
MEDIUM-HIGH (70%)	MEDIUM-HIGH REHEAT ROAST	7
MEDIUM (50%)	MEDIUM BAKE HIGH DEFROST DEFROST	5
LOW (30%)	SIMMER STEW LOW DEFROST	3
WARM (10%)	LOW KEEP WARM	1
		*100% power is automatic.

The number of "Power Level Settings" available on microwave ovens varies from model to model. The names given to these different power levels also vary.

This chart will help you identify the names and power level settings on your microwave oven with the power levels called for in recipes throughout this book.

PRECAUTIONS TO AVOID POSSIBLE EXPOSURE TO EXCESSIVE MICROWAVE ENERGY

Do not attempt to operate the oven with the door open since open door operation can result in harmful exposure to microwave energy. It is important not to defeat or tamper with the safety interlocks.

Do not place any object between the oven front face and the door or allow soil or cleaner residue to accumulate on sealing surfaces.

Do not operate the oven if it is damaged. It is par-ticularly important that the oven door close properly and that there is no damage to the (1) door (bent), (2) hinges and latches (broken or loosened), (3) door seals and sealing surfaces.

The oven should not be adjusted or repaired by anyone except properly qualified service personnel.

Do not attempt to operate oven with temperature probe assembly caught in door (on models equipped with probe).

4

Contents

Introduction to microwave cooking

Quick, convenient, clean and cool. That's what microwave cooking is all about. Add to those factors that the microwave oven is also economical and energy efficient, and you've got the perfect kitchen appliance.

It's quick and convenient! The microwave will save you hours in the kitchen. Most foods will be cooked in just minutes or even seconds as compared to the conventional methods. The microwave is ideal for today's fast-paced lifestyles.

It's clean! Microwave cooking puts an end to messy ovens, range tops and spattered walls. Spills or spatters do not get baked on the inside surfaces of the microwave oven. If they do happen, simply wipe them clean with a damp cloth. Cleanup time is reduced because you can prepare, cook and serve many foods in just one container.

It's cool! The only heat in a microwave oven comes from the food itself. The air inside a microwave oven remains at room temperature and may warm just slightly as the food gets hot. You won't heat up the whole kitchen with your microwave.

It's economical and energy efficient! Saving energy is a big concern today. Most of us are looking for any way possible to save energy because that means saving dollars as well. Much of microwave cooking is a one-step process. You'll save energy both in the quick operation of the microwave oven as well as in cleanup.

MICROWAVE OVEN 170 WATTS

CONVENTIONAL RANGE 1,000 WATTS

Approximate Energy Consumption: **Hamburgers** (1-lb., 4 patties)

An artist's concept of how microwa enter the oven, th bounce back off

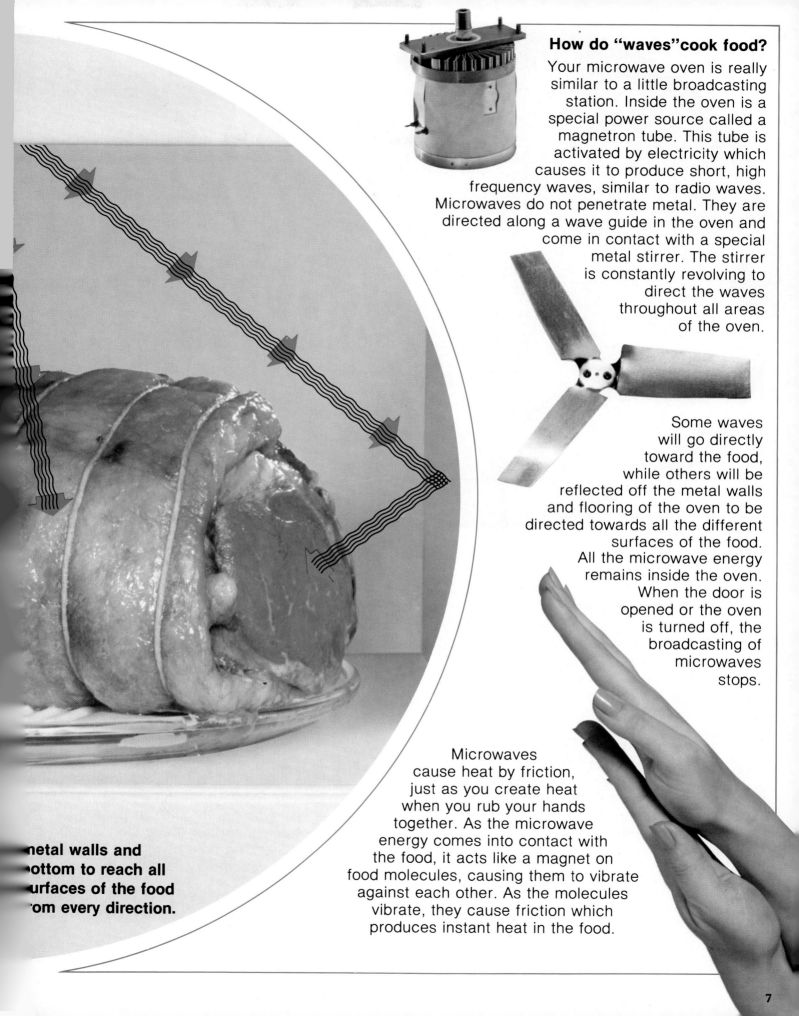

How do "waves" cook food?

Your microwave oven is really similar to a little broadcasting station. Inside the oven is a special power source called a magnetron tube. This tube is activated by electricity which causes it to produce short, high frequency waves, similar to radio waves. Microwaves do not penetrate metal. They are directed along a wave guide in the oven and come in contact with a special metal stirrer. The stirrer is constantly revolving to direct the waves throughout all areas of the oven.

Some waves will go directly toward the food, while others will be reflected off the metal walls and flooring of the oven to be directed towards all the different surfaces of the food. All the microwave energy remains inside the oven. When the door is opened or the oven is turned off, the broadcasting of microwaves stops.

Microwaves cause heat by friction, just as you create heat when you rub your hands together. As the microwave energy comes into contact with the food, it acts like a magnet on food molecules, causing them to vibrate against each other. As the molecules vibrate, they cause friction which produces instant heat in the food.

...metal walls and ...ottom to reach all ...urfaces of the food ...om every direction.

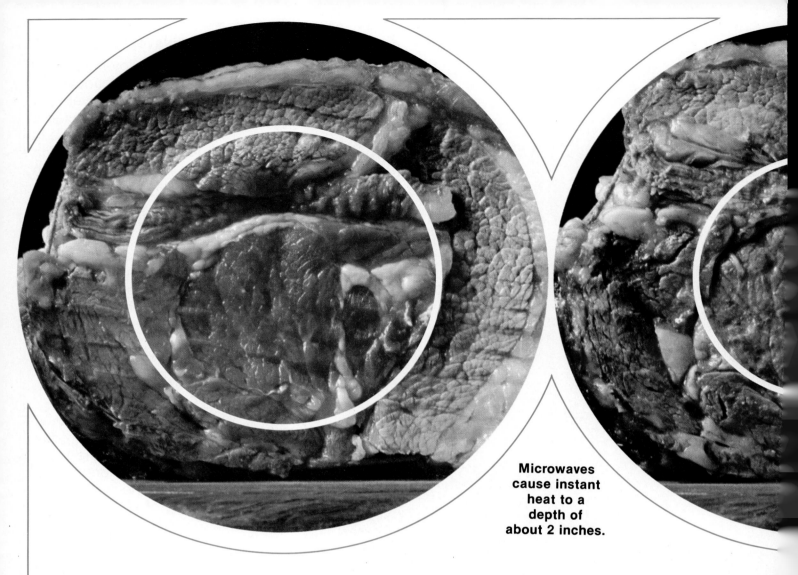

Microwaves cause instant heat to a depth of about 2 inches.

A common misconception

It is a common misconception that foods cooked in the microwave cook from the inside out. Actually, microwaves cause molecules to vibrate only to a depth of about 2 inches in food, depending on the differences in resistance and different types of food. Heat from these vibrating molecules then moves toward the center of the food, and the food becomes cooked.

Foods of small size and low density tend to cook throughout at the same time. In larger, more dense foods, the cooking is started at the outer edges and heat is conducted to the center.

The importance of "standing time"

An important difference between microwave and conventional cooking is the need for "standing time." In microwave cooking, a standing time is usually recommended.

During this standing time, the internal heat causes foods to finish cooking. Temperatures will even out throughout the food. Meat actually is further tenderized during this time. Standing time helps you to avoid overcooking which may tend to toughen some foods.

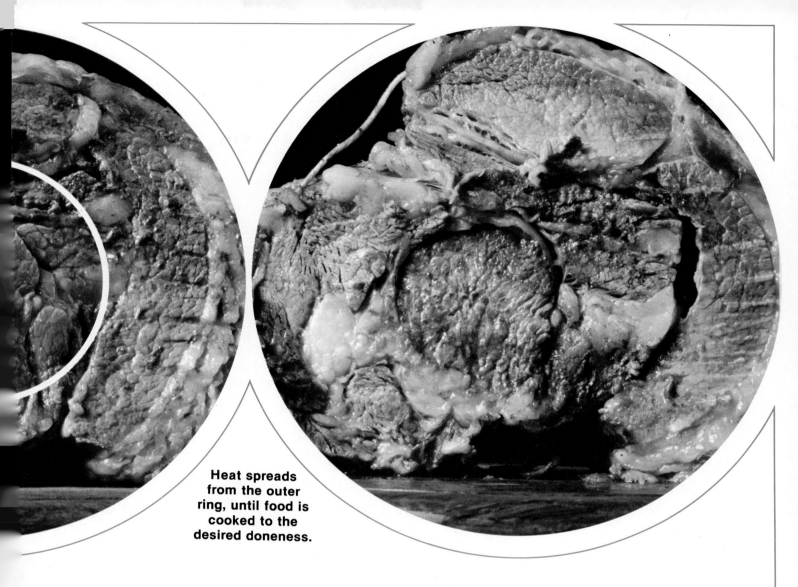

Heat spreads from the outer ring, until food is cooked to the desired doneness.

It's more than an "oven!"

Your microwave oven is called an "oven" but it is really much more than an oven. It can be used for many of the kinds of cooking you are used to doing on top of the range as well as inside the conventional oven.

But in the microwave oven, it is the microwave effect on food molecules which causes the food to heat and to cook — not food contact with a hot pan or hot dry air.

You can boil water, cook bacon, saute or steam foods, make cakes, breads or roasts — all in the microwave!

Life will be easier

The microwave oven will make your life easier. You'll be learning some new cooking techniques as you use this cookbook, and you'll be pleasantly surprised to discover how microwave cooking helps you save energy. In no time at all, you'll even be preparing foods that you might have hesitated to cook in the conventional manner. The microwave oven makes it easy to add variety to your day-to-day meal planning.

9

The right utensils for microwave cooking

Many of the dishes and utensils in your kitchen are usable in the microwave oven, so you don't have to buy all new cookware. But many new utensils have been specially designed to make microwave cooking easier. Microwaves pass through most materials but not through any metal, so metal containers and utensils should not be used in the microwave oven.

Many new utensils are specially designed to make microwave cooking easier. Pictured above are helpful utensils for cooking meats, for baking and other microwave cooking.

Wooden tools are very helpful. Unlike metal tools, they can be left in the microwave oven when frequent stirring is necessary.

Dinnerware. Much of today's dinnerware is marked for use in the microwave. When in doubt, use the dish test (see page 12). Don't use metal-trimmed dishes and check to see if a plate may have been signed or decorated with a metal-base paint.

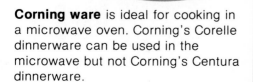

Corning ware is ideal for cooking in a microwave oven. Corning's Corelle dinnerware can be used in the microwave but not Corning's Centura dinnerware.

Glass oven ware. Glassware used in conventional ovens is also good for microwave ovens because it allows microwaves to pass through into the food.

Some plastics are specially made and marked for microwave cooking. Others will become deformed when the food gets hot. Therefore they should only be used for heating foods to serving temperature, not for cooking.

Pottery cookware, without metal trim, is usually fine for microwave cooking. Use the dish test to be sure. Extra thick or colored pottery may require a little extra cooking time.

...eramics and porcelain are usable. ...e sure not to use any with metallic ...ms or decoration. If the ware is extra ...ick you may have to add a little extra ...ooking time.

Seashells. Because microwaves pass through seashells, they're great for cooking seafood casseroles or hot seafood appetizers.

Wood and straw. Wooden dishes and straw baskets can be used for quick reheating of foods but aren't recommended for baking and cooking.

Paper ware. You probably never thought of paper ware as cookware but paper plates, paper towels, wax paper, paper napkins, frozen food cartons, plastic wrap and meat-packing paperboard are all okay for microwave cooking.

Microwave browning dishes and griddles are specially made to let you add a crisp, browned finish to your microwave cooking. The use of a 10'' browning dish and 12'' griddle are described in our recipes.

TESTING DISHES

Place the dish in the microwave along with a glass measuring cup half full of water. Heat on High (100%) for one minute. If the dish feels hot, you shouldn't use it. If it's just slightly warm, you can use it for reheating but not for cooking. If the dish is room temperature, it's okay for microwave cooking.

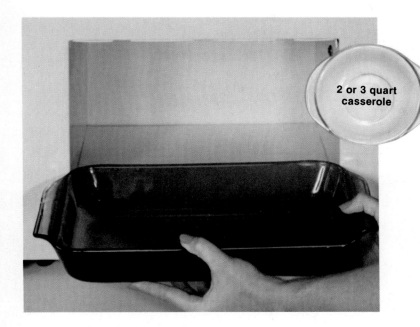

2 or 3 quart casserole

10¼ x 8³/₈ x 2½ inch Corning ware

12 inch pizza or quiche dish

To Substitute Baking Dish Sizes

Our recipes sometimes call for an 11¾ x 7½ x 1¾ inch baking dish. If you have a Space-Saver microwave oven or one with a turntable, instead of this size dish you can substitute: a 10¼ x 8³/₈ x 2½ inch Corning ware dish, a 2 or 3 quart casserole, or a 12 inch round pizza dish or quiche dish. Stir or rearrange foods if necessary.

Do not use metal pots, pans or utensils, metal-trimmed, metallic-decorated or metallic-labeled dishes, foil or foil-lined trays in the microwave oven because microwaves will not pass through these materials to properly cook the food. This includes all kinds of metal: gold, silver, brass, platinum, copper, aluminum or cast iron. Watch for hidden metal such as screws, wire inside paper twisters or metal inside wicker handles.

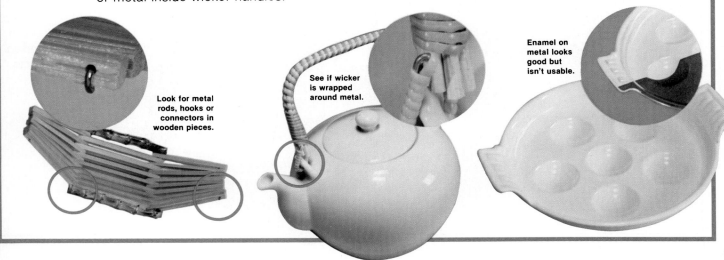

Look for metal rods, hooks or connectors in wooden pieces.

See if wicker is wrapped around metal.

Enamel on metal looks good but isn't usable.

Paper Products are Useful Utensils

Paper products make excellent companions to microwave cooking. Different kinds of paper help obtain different results in cooking. For example, if you want to retain more moisture, you'll probably be covering with plastic wrap.

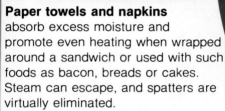

Paper towels and napkins absorb excess moisture and promote even heating when wrapped around a sandwich or used with such foods as bacon, breads or cakes. Steam can escape, and spatters are virtually eliminated.

Do not use colored paper towel or napkins as the color may tend to bleed onto the food.

Waxed paper. Using a light cover of waxed paper when cooking lets you hold in heat and retain some moisture. For fast, even heating use waxed paper for covering some foods.

When less moisture is desired, you may be using waxed paper. Paper towels and napkins are used for heating and serving foods, and as covers for absorbing moisture and cutting down spatters during cooking.

Plastic wrap. A tight covering of plastic wrap allows you to steam and tenderize food. It helps to pleat the plastic wrap covering to allow room for the steam to expand. When removing plastic lift carefully from far end to allow steam to escape.

Cooking bags. When used for large cuts of meat, roasts, turkey or chicken, these bags hold in moisture. Sometimes the food may cook even faster. Use string or cut a strip of plastic from the open end to use as a tie for the bag. Halfway through cooking slash a small "X" in the bag to allow some steam to escape.

Boilable freezer bags. These bags hold in moisture so make a small "X" slash in the bag to allow some steam to escape.

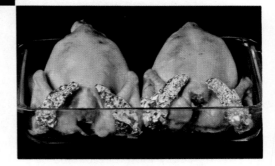

Aluminum foil. Small pieces of aluminum foil are used to protect some spots on food from overcooking. This shielding technique is also used in defrosting. This shielding technique is illustrated whenever appropriate throughout this book.

Using the temperature probe

The temperature probe lets you enjoy carefree cooking and heating without guesswork for many foods. Made of special material, the probe senses the temperature of the food and turns the microwave oven off when the preset temperature is reached. There is no need to set a cooking time.

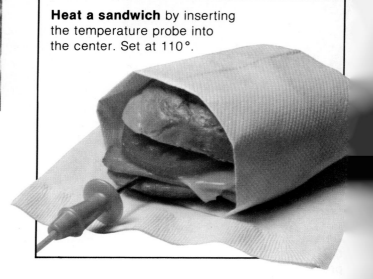

Heat a sandwich by inserting the temperature probe into the center. Set at 110°.

Insert the temperature probe at least 1 inch into food. Ideally the probe should be as horizontal as possible, regardless of the shape or size of the food. Defrost food first. The probe could break if you try to insert it into hard frozen food. When in use, the probe should not be touching plastic or paper, nor the walls, door or floor of the microwave oven. Do not use the probe with a browning dish. The handle of the probe may get hot during cooking, so use a pot holder when removing.

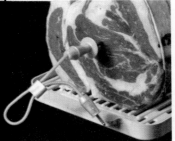

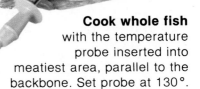

Roast meat to rare, medium or well done with the temperature probe. The probe should be inserted into the center of the meatiest area. The probe tip should not touch bone nor fat.

Cook whole fish with the temperature probe inserted into meatiest area, parallel to the backbone. Set probe at 130°.

Heat soups or beverages with the temperature probe set at 150° to 160°. For milk-base beverages, set at 130° to 140°.

Warm sauces, gravies or dips with the probe. Set the probe at 130° to 140° for sauces, gravies and dips.

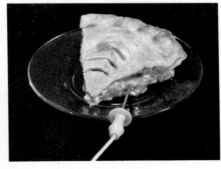

Warm baked goods with the temperature probe inserted as horizontally as possible with tip near the center. Set probe at 110° to 120°.

Have hot syrup for pancakes or waffles or toppings for sundaes. Heat in the container or pour syrup or topping into a glass measuring cup. Insert probe and set temperature at 130° to 140°.

Reheat vegetables or leftover mashed potatoes with the probe set at 140° to 150°.

Reheat precooked casseroles or cook casseroles with the temperature probe. Insert probe so tip is in the center of the casserole. Follow recipe for probe setting when cooking casseroles. When reheating, set the probe at 150° to 160°. Stir once during cooking.

Using the
Power levels

The various settings on microwave ovens are called "Power Levels" (rather than "Temperature Settings" as on conventional ovens). The number of "Power Level" settings available and the kinds of controls used, will vary on different models of microwave ovens.

 **Some models use knobs or dials:** turning the pointer adjusts the "Power Level" to the desired setting. As many as seven settings are indicated on some models.

Other models use solid state "Touch" controls: by 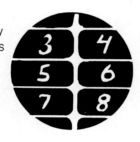 touching the numbered pads on a panel the desired "Percentage of Power Level" is selected. These models have 10 power settings from 0 to 90%; 100% is automatic.

The different power level settings are used for cooking different kinds of foods, as well as for different cooking methods. Therefore the additional power levels available on some models provide additional cooking flexibility, but do not change the basic principles of microwave cooking.

To make it easier to use the recipes in this book the "Power Levels" specified for each recipe have been limited to the five basic settings that are available on most models of microwave ovens:

HIGH (100%) *This is the full power, fastest cooking setting. Generally used for cooking fish, fruits, gravies, sauces, puddings, most soups, cookies, candy, sandwiches and vegetables.*

MEDIUM-HIGH (70%) *Uses 70% of the oven's power, for foods which will require more gentle cooking such as meats, cakes, poultry and some soups.*

MEDIUM (50%) *Uses approximately half the full power when slower cooking and tenderizing is desired for such foods as stews and less tender cuts of meat, eggs, cheese, rice and pasta.*

LOW (30%) *Used when only one-third of the power is required for the delicate kinds of food that need more cooking time. Use this setting for softening cheese and butter, cooking custards and for drying fruits and vegetables. You'll defrost most foods at this power level.*

WARM (10%) *This setting is used primarily for keeping cooked foods warm, for up to a half-hour without causing overcooking.*

Different models of microwave ovens frequently use different words on the Selector Controls to describe the Power Level Settings. Use this reference chart to find the Power Level descriptions on your microwave oven which are equivalent to the five Power Level settings specified in the recipes in this book.

Power Levels used in the recipes	Equivalent Settings on various Selector Controls	Power Level Settings on Touch Controls
HIGH (100%)	**NORMAL**	*
MEDIUM-HIGH (70%)	**MEDIUM-HIGH REHEAT ROAST**	7
MEDIUM (50%)	**MEDIUM BAKE HIGH DEFROST DEFROST**	5
LOW (30%)	**SIMMER STEW LOW DEFROST**	3
WARM (10%)	**LOW KEEP WARM**	1
		*100% power is automatic.

TO TEST COOKING TIMES

The cooking times recommended in our recipes were all tested on one or more of our microwave ovens. However house power can vary in different locations of the country, during peak use times or during weather extremes. Such differences in the power supply going to your microwave oven can cause changes in the cooking times required.

It's not difficult to test the cooking time required in your microwave oven against the times used in the recipes in this book.

To make the test, place a measuring cup of room temperature water in your microwave oven. Microwave on HIGH (100%) for 2½ to 3 minutes:

If the water boils within this time, your cooking times should be the same as those we have used in this book.

If the water boils in less time, you'll be able to use slightly less time.

If it takes longer for the water to boil, your cooking times may have to be a bit longer.

When cooking, it's always a good idea to check for doneness at the minimum cooking time. That way you can avoid overcooking or allow extra cooking time if necessary.

Time and energy-saving
Menu planning ideas

Remember when you first began cooking and the hardest thing was getting all the food hot and ready for serving at the same time? With the microwave, you'll soon be a master at quickly preparing whole meals.

When menu planning, keep in mind the importance of good nutrition. Select food from the various food groups. Foods of different color, texture and flavor add appetite and eye-appeal.

Plan your cooking so all foods will not need last-minute attention. Set the table first. Gather ingredients and prepare for cooking.

The first foods to cook are those that need the longest cooking and standing time, or that stay hot longest, such as meats or potatoes. Then move on to those foods such as vegetables and rolls that need the least amount of cooking and standing time.

You can prepare desserts and sauces or foods that reheat quickly earlier in the day when you have extra time. Desserts can be reheated quickly in the microwave while you're clearing away the dinner dishes.

Turn the page for more menu planning ideas.

Let's start cooking!

BREAKFAST FOR 1:

Orange Juice
Hot Oatmeal (page 147)
Sweet Roll (page 51)
Coffee (page 47)

1. Assemble all ingredients and utensils.
2. Set the table and pour the juice.
3. Cook the oatmeal (1½ to 2½ minutes).
4. Heat water for instant coffee (2 to 3 minutes).
5. Heat the sweet roll (15 seconds) while placing food on the table.

BREAKFAST FOR 2:

Hot Breakfast
Grapefruit (page 99)
Scrambled Eggs (page 76)
Bacon (page 139)
Toast
Hot Chocolate (page 49)

1. Assemble ingredients and utensils.
2. Set the table.
3. Measure and prepare foods for cooking.
4. Cook six slices of bacon (4½ to 5½ minutes).
5. Remove bacon from microwave and cover with foil. While bacon is standing, cook four eggs (3 to 3½ minutes).
6. While eggs are standing, cook grapefruit (2 to 3 minutes) and toast bread in your toaster.
7. Heat hot chocolate in microwave (2 to 3 minutes).
8. If necessary, reheat bacon (15 to 30 seconds) while placing food on table.

BRUNCH FOR 4:

Tomato Juice
Eggs Benedict (page 77)
Sour Cream Streusel
Coffeecake (page 52)
Coffee or Tea (page 47)

1. Prepare coffeecake and Hollandaise Sauce (page 107) for Eggs Benedict. If desired do this early in the morning or the day before and keep Hollandaise Sauce refrigerated.
2. Assemble all ingredients and utensils.
3. Set table and pour tomato juice.
4. Measure and prepare foods for cooking.
5. Heat water for instant coffee (6 to 7 min.).
6. Poach four eggs (3½ to 4 minutes) and do English muffins in toaster or broiler.
7. Heat ham on muffins (1½ to 2 minutes) while eggs stand.
8. Reheat sauce (15 to 30 seconds).
9. Assemble Eggs Benedict and place food on the table.

LUNCH FOR 4 TO 6:

Chicken Divan
Sandwich (page 172)
Relishes - carrots, celery, radish
Quick Ambrosia (page 98)
Lemon Meringue Pie (page 149)

1. Make pie early in the day and refrigerate after cooling.
2. Assemble all ingredients and utensils.
3. Set the table.
4. Measure and prepare foods for cooking.
5. Heat sandwiches (8 to 10 minutes).
6. Heat fruit ambrosia (3 to 4½ minutes).
7. Place food on table.

DINNER FOR 4:

Roast Beef (page 129)
Baked Potato (page 188)
Broccoli with Cheese
Sauce (pages 185 and 107)
Tossed Salad
Rolls (page 51)
Upside-Down Cake (page 63)

1. Assemble all ingredients and utensils.
2. Set the table. Toss salad and refrigerate.
3. Prepare upside-down cake (7 to 10 minutes) or prepare cake earlier in the day.
4. Place 3 pound beef roast on trivet, cover and cook (about 30 minutes).
5. While meat is cooking, scrub and pierce potatoes. Clean broccoli and place in dish. Prepare cheese sauce (unless prepared earlier in the day) for cooking.
6. Remove roast from oven and tent with foil. While meat is standing, cook the potatoes (12 to 14 minutes).
7. Remove potatoes from oven and wrap with foil. Allow to stand. Cook broccoli (8 to 10 minutes).
8. While broccoli is standing, reheat sauce (15 to 30 seconds) or cook sauce (3¼ to 4½ minutes).
9. Heat rolls and place food on the table.

DINNER FOR 4 TO 6:

Turkey and Rice Bake (page 163)
Asparagus (page 185)
Tomato slice with mayonnaise
Italian Bread Slice
Baked Apple with
Cinnamon Candies (page 97)

1. Assemble all ingredients and utensils.
2. Set table. Prepare salad and refrigerate.
3. Measure and prepare foods for cooking.
4. Cook casserole (8 to 10 minutes).
5. Remove casserole from oven and cover with foil. While casserole stands, cook asparagus (6 to 8 minutes).
6. Place foods on table. While eating, cook apples (8 to 10 minutes) and allow to stand.
7. Serve apples.

Converting a standard recipe for microwave cooking.

Many of your favorite recipes can be converted to microwave cooking.

The most reliable way to convert a standard recipe is to find a similar microwave recipe or to look for microwave cooking instructions for the main ingredients of your recipe.

Follow the microwave recipe for cooking techniques, power levels, times, seasoning amounts, dish sizes and covering procedures.

If you cannot find a similar microwave recipe, follow these steps:

1 **Check for any special instructions** for the main ingredient of your recipe.

2 **Reduce liquid by about one-half** or add more thickening since there is less evaporation in the microwave. Sometimes liquid may even be omitted.

3 **Use less seasoning.** Usually one-half the seasoning will do. You can adjust to taste after cooking.

4 **Any cooking oils or fats may be reduced** or may not be needed at all because they do not evaporate in the microwave as they would in conventional cooking. Fats tend to attract microwaves away from the food and may cause food to cook longer. Remove any excess grease when possible.

5 **You may wish to precook hamburger** or other meats first and then drain them. This avoids excess fat as well as the overcooking of other foods in the recipe.

6 **Reduce the cooking time** to about:
one-fourth for High (100%)
one-third for Medium-High (70%)
one-half for Medium (50%)
three-fourths for Low (30%).

7 **Substitute instant or quick cooking ingredients** for those ingredients which may take longer to cook than other foods in the recipe.

8 **Some stirring or rearranging** of food may be necessary during cooking. Stir occasionally when your recipe calls for constant stirring or when you would naturally stir.

---

4 omit or reduce cooking oil.

6 reduce cooking time to one-fourth.

8 stir or rearrange.

Here's what's cookin':   SLOPPY JOES   Serves: 6-8

2 tablespoons oil
1½ lbs. ground beef
½ cup chopped onion
½ cup chopped celery
½ cup chopped green peppers

½ cup catsup
¼ cup water
1 T. Worcestershire sauce
1/8 tsp. red pepper sauce
1 teaspoon salt

Heat oil in 10 inch skillet. Add meat and onion. Cook until meat is lightly browned. Drain. Stir in remaining ingredients. Cover and cook on low heat for 20 to 25 minutes or until vegetables are just tender. Stir frequently.

2 omit liquid

3 use less seasoning: 1½ tsp. Worcestershire, ½ tsp. salt, dash of pepper

1 cook until slightly pink in center.

Some recipes such as cakes, candies, meat loaves or main dish casseroles may need only a power level and time conversion but no changes in ingredients.

Whenever you convert a recipe, record all changes for future use.

There are a few foods which you will probably prefer to cook in the conventional manner because they are difficult to get satisfactory results when using the microwave. These foods include:

1 **Fried foods** which tend not to get crisp. Also do not deep fat fry in the microwave. Crusty foods such as popovers or French fries tend to get soggy.

2 **Yeast bread recipes** are difficult to convert. It is best to use only those recipes which are specially formulated for microwave cooking.

3 **Souffles** are very delicate and take a long time to make. For easier cooking make souffles in the conventional way.

Be your own test cook. After preparing and serving the converted recipe, you can put a proven microwave recipe in your file.

Here's what's cookin':   SLOPPY JOES   Serves: 6-8

1½ lbs. ground beef
½ cup chopped onion
½ cup chopped celery
½ cup chopped green peppers

½ cup catsup
1½ tsp. Worcestershire sauce
½ teaspoon salt
Dash of red pepper sauce

Place meat and onion in a casserole or baking dish. Cook on HIGH (100%) until meat is slightly pink in center. Stir halfway through cooking. Drain. Stir in remaining ingredients. Cover. Cook on HIGH for 5 to 7 minutes or until vegetables are just tender. Stir occasionally.

Defrosting with the microwave oven

Defrosting foods is a big time-saving advantage of the microwave oven. If you've ever forgotten to plan a meal far

There are special techniques to learn about defrosting in a microwave oven. These pretty ice penguins help to illustrate what will happen inside frozen foods during defrosting. Remember that ice crystals react rather slowly to microwave energy, but water has a high attraction and heats rapidly. Therefore when the ice crystals start to melt, the water that is formed reacts much faster than the remaining ice.

enough ahead to allow time for meat or another main dish to defrost, you will really appreciate the microwave.

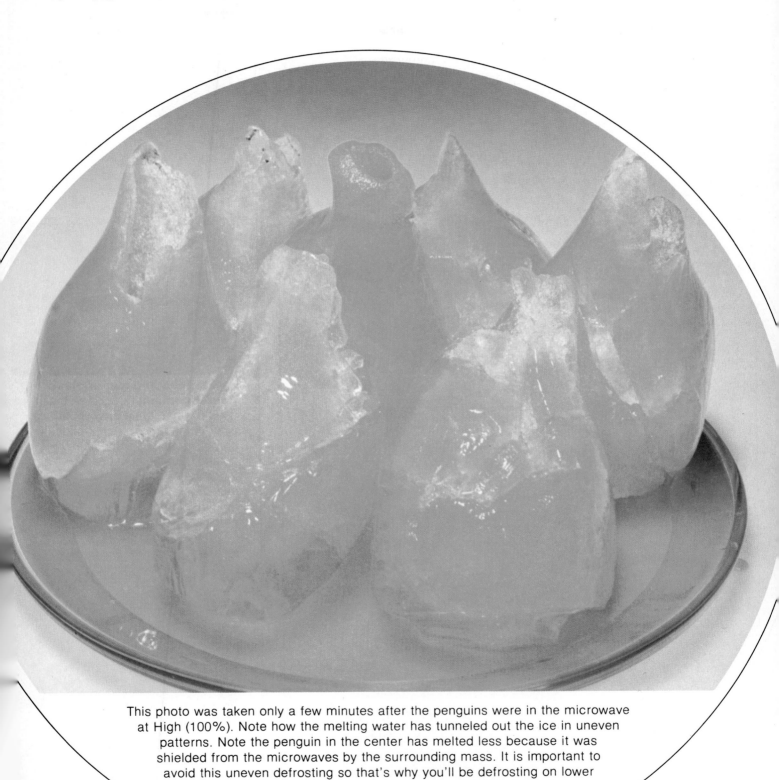

This photo was taken only a few minutes after the penguins were in the microwave at High (100%). Note how the melting water has tunneled out the ice in uneven patterns. Note the penguin in the center has melted less because it was shielded from the microwaves by the surrounding mass. It is important to avoid this uneven defrosting so that's why you'll be defrosting on lower power levels. Study the next pages and the specific defrosting instructions in this cookbook's recipe sections.

DEFROST THOROUGHLY

It is important to thoroughly defrost food before starting to cook. For most food, the Low (30%) power level is recommended for defrosting. At low settings, the microwave oven automatically cycles ''on'' and ''off'' which allows the heat to equalize throughout the food. At high power levels, cooking can start on the outside before food is completely defrosted on the inside.

At High (100%) power, this hamburger patty shows signs of cooking before being thoroughly defrosted.

Attempting to defrost at Medium (50%) power still shows signs that cooking has started before meat is thoroughly defrosted.

Using Low (30%) power allows you to thoroughly defrost meat without starting the cooking process.

FROM FREEZER TO THE MICROWAVE

Frozen food in boilable plastic bags can be both defrosted and heated for serving in the microwave. Make an ''X'' slash in the bag to allow steam to escape.

Freeze food in paper or plastic freezer containers such as those used for margarine or whipped toppings. In the microwave, foods can be defrosted and sometimes reheated in these containers. Greasy foods may cause some plastics to become deformed if the food gets too hot. Do not use foil or foil-lined containers.

You can freeze foods in those special dishes which are designed to be used directly ''from freezer to oven to table'' in your microwave oven. Foods in such dishes can be defrosted and heated to serving temperature.

DEFROSTING TIPS

It helps to flex frozen food in plastic pouches while defrosting. This distributes heat and makes the defrosting faster.

When defrosting meat, remove any insulated packaging such as Styrofoam trays or paper liners which are used to absorb juices. Such paper products may become saturated with moisture so they will draw microwave energy away from the meat and slow down defrosting.

Remove any metal containers deeper than ¾ inch. Transfer foods in such containers to microwave safe dishes for defrosting.

Stir or break foods apart to distribute heat and speed defrosting.

When defrosting ground meat, it helps to remove meat on the outer edges. This meat could start cooking before the rest of the meat has finished defrosting.

Pouring liquid from foods, such as frozen poultry in a plastic bag will speed up the defrosting time.

Use small pieces of foil to shield any tender parts or spots which may be getting warm during defrosting.

Cover foods with wax paper during defrosting for more even heating and some moisture retention.

When you finish defrosting food in the microwave oven, it may still be slightly icy. You can complete the defrosting by holding such foods as frozen fish or poultry under cold, running water. When properly defrosted and ready for cooking, food should be cool, soft, moist and glossy.

Convenience foods

Convenience foods can be more convenient than ever when heated in your microwave oven. These foods can be brought to serving temperature in less time than would be spent heating in the conventional manner. In fact, many brands now include special microwave instructions right on the package.

If convenience foods come in a thick, metal tray, the food should be transferred to a microwave safe dish such as a casserole or baking dish. TV dinner trays less than ¾ inch thick and frozen juice cans are exceptions.

Convenience foods in boilable plastic pouches can be reheated on a plate. Slash an "X" in the top to allow steam to escape.

Remove the metal lid from one end of a can of frozen juice. Defrost on Medium (50%). Concentrate should be soft and cool after defrosting. If concentrate becomes warm, vitamin C may be lost.

CONVENIENCE FOOD CHART		
Item	Power Level	Cooking Time
Canned Meat or Poultry Main Dishes under 16 ounces over 16 ounces	 High (100%) High (100%)	 4 to 6 minutes 8 to 10 minutes (or temperature probe can be used, set at 150° to 160°)
Frozen Fried Chicken Pieces 2 pounds	 High (100%)	 8 to 10 minutes
Frozen Fruits 10 to 12 ounces	 High (100%)	 6 to 8 minutes
Frozen Juices 6 ounces 12 ounces 16 ounces	 Medium (50%) Medium (50%) Medium (50%)	 2 to 3 minutes 3 to 4 minutes 4 to 6 minutes
Frozen Macaroni & Cheese (or other Pasta Dishes) 12 ounces 32 ounces	 High (100%) High (100%)	 8 to 10 minutes 14 to 16 minutes
Frozen Meat or Poultry Main Dishes 5 to 8 ounces 8 to 12 ounces 12 to 16 ounces 16 to 32 ounces	 High (100%) High (100%) High (100%) High (100%)	 3 to 5 minutes 5 to 8 minutes 8 to 10 minutes 10 to 20 minutes
Frozen Vegetables (In Sauce, Au Gratin, Scalloped or Stuffed) 10 to 12 ounces	 High (100%)	 7 to 9 minutes

Stir and cover foods not in boilable bags.

HOW TO MICROWAVE A TV DINNER

Remove TV dinner from its box. Then remove foil covering from the dinner. We do not recommend heating three-course dinners in the microwave.

Cover dinner with plastic wrap, pleated to allow steam to expand. Unless the foil tray is more than ¾ inch deep, it is not necessary to transfer the food to another dish. It's best to remove porous foods such as brownies or cornbread or sweets such as puddings. Return them to the dinner during the last 15 to 20 seconds of heating.

Microwave on High (100%). Most dinners will thaw and heat to serving temperature in 5 to 7 minutes. Larger portion dinners may take 12 to 15 minutes. When the tray becomes warm on the bottom, the dinner is thoroughly heated. Allow 2 minutes standing time before eating.

You can heat a TV dinner even more quickly if you do transfer the foods to a microwave safe dish.

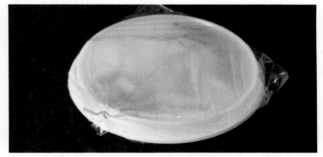

Make your own TV dinners. Use a divided plastic plate or one of the special divided microwave plates which have their own lids. Arrange food on plate. Cover with lid or plastic wrap. Secure with foil or plastic bag for freezer storage. Remove foil, metal twister or bag (but not plastic wrap or lid) before heating. You can heat these frozen dinners to serving temperature in 3 to 5 minutes on High (100%). Times may vary according to the food you select.

Reheating Techniques

Reheat foods in the microwave without loss of quality, moisture, flavor or texture. Now leftovers will taste fresh, almost like they have just been prepared for the first time.

Most reheating is done using High (100%) power. For more delicate foods, you may wish to reheat on a lower power setting.

When reheating meats, remember that you don't want to restart the cooking process unless you want the meat to be more fully cooked than before it was reheated. You'll also find meat reheats more quickly when sliced into smaller pieces.

Small amounts of food will reheat more quickly than large amounts of food. It's faster to reheat casseroles by spreading the food out in a shallow dish.

Foods in a dish should be of the same starting temperature for reheating. A plate of room temperature food will take about 1 to 1¼ minutes to reheat; a refrigerator temperature plate will take 1½ to 2 minutes. Arrange foods so pieces that take longer to reheat are on the outside while more tender food is towards the inside.

It helps to cover foods when reheating. Waxed paper works best for a plate of food while vegetables or a casserole may benefit most by a covering of plastic wrap or a tight fitting lid.

Breads and sugary foods such as desserts and rolls reheat very quickly and can easily be overcooked. When reheating foods, add these items during the last 15 to 30 seconds.

Stirring foods occasionally during reheating will help to distribute the heat throughout the food and speed the reheating time.

You can add extra flavor and speed up reheating by adding a tablespoon of butter (or margarine) to pasta, rice or vegetables. Adding sauces to meats has the same effect. This is because moisture and fat tend to attract microwave energy to foods.

Use the temperature probe for fast, even reheating. Set it at 150° to 160°.

Appetizers & Hors d'oeuvres

Guests will rave over the hot appetizers you can make in minutes. These treats are easily prepared in advance, to be heated when the company arrives. Or let guests join in the fun and warm their own.

Pierce the thick outer membrane *of oysters and escargots to allow steam to escape and to prevent spattering.*

Cover oysters and escargots completely *with sauce to prevent them from popping out of their shells.*

Place shellfish in a circle *with small tender parts toward the center for even heating without overcooking. Use lower power levels and slowly cook clams, oysters and escargots. You might try using the new microwave paper plates rather than a glass or ceramic serving dish.*

LOBSTER DAINTIES OR ROCK SHRIMP

Power Level: HIGH [100%]
Total Cooking Time: 2½ to
3½ minutes

16 lobster dainties (or rock shrimp)

1. Cut through soft shell side. Place tails, hard shell side up, in a circle with tips toward center on a serving plate. Cover with plastic wrap.

2. Microwave on HIGH (100%) for 2½ to 3½ minutes or until meat is opaque and shell is pink.

3. If desired, serve with melted butter or chili sauce.

Recipe yield: 4 servings

Shellfish

The delicate flavors of shellfish are most delicious when steamed in the microwave oven. Do them in their shells, or in a dish covered with pleated plastic wrap. Cook and serve immediately.

OYSTERS DENNIE

Power Level: HIGH [100%] and
MEDIUM [50%]
Total Cooking Time: 5¾ to
7½ minutes

Sauce:
5 tablespoons butter (or margarine)
1 cup chopped celery
¼ cup chopped onion
¼ cup finely chopped green pepper
1 bottle (12 ounces) chili sauce
1 teaspoon brown sugar

Oysters:
2 cups oysters
2 cups milk
1 tablespoon butter (or margarine)
Dash of salt
Dash of pepper
12 to 18 oyster or clam shells

1. Place 5 tablespoons butter, celery, onion and green pepper in a 1 quart casserole. Microwave on HIGH (100%) for 3 to 4 minutes or until vegetables are tender.

2. Stir in chili sauce and brown sugar. Set aside.

3. Pierce oyster membranes. Combine oysters, milk, remaining butter, salt and pepper in a 1½ quart casserole. Microwave on HIGH (100%) for 2 to 2½ minutes or until edges of oysters curl.

4. Place 1 or 2 oysters and 1 teaspoon broth in each shell. Top each with 1 tablespoon sauce making sure oysters are completely covered.

5. Microwave 6 at a time in a circle on MEDIUM (50%) for 45 seconds to 1 minute or until hot and bubbly. Repeat with remaining oysters.

Recipe yield: 4 to   6 servings or
                12 to 18 oysters

ESCARGOTS

Power Level: HIGH [100%] and
LOW [30%]
Total Cooking Time: About 1¼ min-
utes per plate

⅓ cup butter (or margarine)
¼ cup lemon juice
1 tablespoon instant minced onion
1 tablespoon chopped parsley
½ teaspoon minced garlic
1 can (4 ounces) medium size
escargots (about 24) with shells

1. Place butter, lemon juice, onion, parsley and garlic in a 2 cup measure. Microwave on HIGH (100%) for 45 seconds to 1 minute or until butter is melted. Stir.

2. Drain and rinse escargots. Fill each shell with a small amount of sauce, place snail in loosely and cover with more sauce. (Do not plug hole with snail).

3. Place 6 snails in a circle on each plate. Microwave, one plate at a time, on LOW (30%) for 35 to 40 seconds.* Repeat with remaining appetizers.

Recipe yield: 4 servings

*Be careful not to overcook because snails will pop out of shells.

CRAB CLAWS

Power Level: HIGH [100%]
Total Cooking Time: 3 to 4 minutes

12 precooked frozen crab claws

1. Place crab claws in a circle with tip toward center on a serving dish. Cove with plastic wrap.

2. Microwave on HIGH (100%) for to 4 minutes or until heated through.

3. If desired, serve with melted butt or chili sauce.

Recipe yield: 3 to 4 servings